Being

A collection of poems

Nick Lewis

Copyright © 2024 Nick Lewis

All rights reserved, including the right to reproduce this book, or portions thereof in any form. No part of this text may be reproduced, transmitted, downloaded, decompiled, reverse engineered, or stored, in any form or introduced into any information storage and retrieval system, in any form or by any means, whether electronic or mechanical without the express written permission of the author.

ISBN: 978-1-917425-64-3

By Way of an Introduction

Included here are some poems written over the years – and I mean many years, given that I am approaching my 80th. Not being at this point a professional writer, poems come to me at times, naturally enough, of emotion, of needing to record feelings, and not to forget them. Some streams here are literally streams: for instance Thames, attempting a poem alongside Alice Oswald's portrayal of the river Dart. From the Cotswolds via London to Oxfordshire and Eynsham where I live with my family now. The place – named poems are partly an attempt to follow Oswald.

My thanks are due to my daughter Zoe, whose idea it was to collect and publish my poetry. In addition, my wife Tricia who patiently supported my efforts, the Eynsham Poetry Circle, led so inspiringly by Jane Spiro, and my dear friend Sue Raikes, who kept the flame going helped by the staff of a certain local café.

Contents

By Way of an Introduction iii
Being 1
I Don't Know Why I'm Here, She Said 3
Haiku 4
It's Not The End Of The World, You Know 5
A poem for Burns Night 7
Long Mead Meadow 8
Looking Upwards 9
Peace Oak in Winter 11
Tank 12
Conduit Lane 13
Coldharbour Lane 14
In The ICU 16
Abbey Street 17
It Might Have Been 18
Gone 19
Ode to the Bath Plug 20
Redemption 21
Sunflowers .... 2?
Fishy February 2
Northmoor ....
Don't stop me ....

Untitled 27
Thames 28
London – 1950s 30
On Seeing Wild Goats on an Island off Mallaig 31
Xtinction Rebellion 32

Being

Not to find the dawn unfolding with me
as I stretch myself from sleep.
Not to be greeted by blinks of reds or golds among the branches
nor every now and then by watchful garden birds.
Not to savour autumn words from Keats or Hardy or Ali Smith
nor to be without the pleasures of communal life
That would be the death of me

And what would fill the gap
once occupied by those images, things, moves or feelings?
Some thing, some thoughts or some one new?
Perhaps a manifesto, an aphorism, a gesture, a quote,
or something blown on the wind?
One less to protest "you do not do this in my name"?
One less name to be ignored by those in receipt of petitions?

No. There will be no gap. We have been overtaken
by those new generations who dance along with their words.
But yes, the wind will carry some pleasures,

some causes joined and yet to be joined.
Something found in those images and those words

I Don't Know Why I'm Here, She Said

I called you at Oaken Holt
You picked up the phone
I don't know why I'm here, you said
Or was it: I don't want to be here?
It amounts to the same awful words – or does it?
You could have been wondering, like Eve:
Who had planted you on the planet
And why?
And why didn't you want to be there?
I had something of a solution to both questions:
Let's sing a song
We'll Meet Again
You sang and I sang and you sang better than me.
We enjoyed it, and we enjoyed each other's company
Together, we were finding the answer

Haiku

I see the Rowan
the greens and reds are sunlit
it should be pictured

It's Not The End Of The World, You Know

There will be no other end of the world
wrote Milosz, *as long as a rose is visited by the bumblebee.*
Tis the gift to wake and breathe the morning air
sang the Shakers as they turned.

It's not the end of world, you know
I said as I sat tight around the stove
with the measles and my sisters.
The world had not ended. We'd all slept the night on it.
Next day, we sat there still, folding in the warmth,
counting the sheet-mica stove windows
and counting the time to the end of quarantine.

Since then, time and time again;
one year it's The Flu, next it's Bird Flu. After that it is the Swine Flu.
One time they call you in, next it's while you wait. The next you have to ask.
Now, there's no jab. 'No vaccine' I am stuck at home.
'You're over sixty years and ten.
It's a virus. Like a limpet mine. Hate's men'.

'You're vulnerable', they say. So I keep away
watch the sun and the rain, paint rainbows and pray
for the carers, read beautiful words, write poetry.

A poem for Burns Night
25 January 2020

Jenny, I see you still

So free of care, I see you still
door cast aside and down the hill,
your flying skirt and mostly legs
a vision of who? – my heart just begs

Silly St Trinians – so full of go?
Happiness brimming, head to toe
or those giggling girls down there in Portwenn?
it takes me back again – and again

oh Jenny dear, we were so young
those days would sing if they could have sung
fair lines of Burns are haling me yon
but those days are past and now foregone

Long Mead Meadow
near Eynsham Oxfordshire

Can you sing happy birthday to a field?
This Meadow is one thousand years old
faint greens, the straw of at least thirty kinds of grass
and precious flowers:
Yellow Rattle, Devil's Bit and the Great Burnet
elder brother of the spicy Pimpernel
could this be an age-old birthday song?
They seek it here, they seek it there
Those farmers seek it everywhere
Is It in heaven or is it in hell?
That damned elusive Pimpernel.
But we are told that the Scarlet Pimpernel
which closes its petals when the sun goes down
has been known for perhaps one thousand years
as the Poor Man's Barometer.
No need for a birthday present then.

Looking Upwards

Most weeks I watch The Repair Shop
enjoying the crafts, the engineering,
the family progeny of the items brought in
a teddy bear that is worse for wear
a clockwork train
they don't make 'em like that anymore
in the main, it is said.
A mandolin that won't work
or a wireless oddly needing wires
but they know, these craftsmen and women,
know how? They nod yes they have the know-how,
the expertise – after all they are paid by the BBC
turning turning, moulding moulding, and hammer, hammer
till their charges are as good as new.
Made to look their age they say – as a reminder.
The owners return
to be reminded, to be amazed
they hoped it might be so – and it is.
Just as they were when they were a child,
their grandmothers, grandfathers, mothers, fathers had use of them.

Do they approve? They wonder all
as they look upwards.

Peace Oak in Winter
Eynsham 2000

Knock knock oak tree:
it's cold outside. It must be warm in there.
What? Central heating's broken down?
Don't think so – your leaves are still quite green.

Your roots, your roots send calories,
Surely they should keep you warm.
But share it out a bit, old girl:
it's cold outside that lovely wrinkled coat.

Tell you what, oak tree why don't we
plant another – you can be mother,
and we'll find some magic mushrooms for those roots.
Now, why not let me inside?

January 2024

Tank

We'd crept from fitful sleep below our flat
momentarily to ignore the distant war
our daughter pulled down the blind and said "what's that?"
A **tank** was parked in the street below our floor
I felt my breakfast drain to my boots – "They've shat
on us for days: we will no longer implore!
We'll blast that tank so the whole street hears
Resistance! That's joy to our ears."

My partner took the kids away
So long as they're safe; but they will be missed
perhaps they'll find a place to play
Will we see them again?
Putin's on my list
of criminals and come their day
I'm sure that they will be kissed
by a death worse than the suffocation
they have meted upon our strangled nation

Conduit Lane

I had been told there was a shortcut into the village
it was called Conduit Lane – sloping downwards
from Clover Place and Back Lane
with walls that looked back
to mediaeval times…
A nun stood there
as if lost in prayer
she faced the wall
still, silent as if she was a sentry
from the 16th century, keeping the faith
since the Abbey was demolished
and has a no need of the waters
for which the Conduit
had been constructed.
We found later that climbing it was a plant
with minute blue-white flowers

Coldharbour Lane
Brixton 1981

Saturday night
Coldharbour Lane: a street where, on a normal day,
the shoppers come for chicken grits and pies and eels
and fish and chips,
where if you're black and out of work
you stand and wait outside the boozer
or the car-hire.
Coldharbour Lane's become a Lane again
where people stroll and size each other up
and up

A lovers Lane, its shopfront image exorcised;
instead we worship one another there
where Africans and young black girls and white ones too
and running boys
and all in clothes that aren't too straight
parade

The street that became a stage
where every act was lit by flames

where we the audience now tread
and, curiously, the costumed stars
intrude

A street retreat, a void from city time
where brick on plastic pleasantly resounds
and fresh reflections struck off rounded
helmet, angled shield
give Autumn night a continental look
where private drivers sniffing trouble hurriedly reverse
leaving alone, bereft, an upturned, fire-blacked Ford
Capri

Tonight's pedestrians, declining cumbous, huddled force,
have time and space to ebb
then flow

Sunday night
Last night there was security in strife
but now I walk through these still watchful streets
in sweaty fear of my companion
– a person who assumes me to be human

In The ICU
Under the influence of morphine in the ICU

Roll Call
"Lewis!"
Present but not present
I am here but not here
I am the same person, but not the same
I have been away
Anywhere else I would have to pay
Lights out: a new world, surgeons standing by, I think.
The top woman had come
to show me the scan.
Under the knife
Drugged, where was my life?
somehow I saw different colours
waving to me: was I dead?
Conjured to ICU
a frighteningly white and bright
new world
in presence of murderous spectators
But with me was a friend – she was called "Nurse"

Abbey Street

Bald becassocked monks processed down here.
Ahead, their humble abbot Aelfric.
Five centuries later in my mind is Abbey Road:
"He got joo joo eyeball
He one holy roller
He got hair down to his knee
Come together, right now, over me"
The procession is in tears
Our Abbey is to be torn down
Our Abbott defrocked
His habit summarily torn down
By order of Henry,
King by divine right.
Then Aelfric spoke: "Keep Calm and Carry On.
Brethren, the people of this village henceforth
Will find and revere those broken stones
From our dear old Abbey"

It Might Have Been

There was no hurry:
At that time, no one hurried along the Kings Road.
Style – looking for something stylish
in the shops, on the street.
What had brought me there?
London had brought me there
Not much else to do, when you're trying to pick up the odd A-level: there might be something: didn't know what,
but London put me there.
I joined the shoppers walking towards: World's End?
⁀owards me was a girl. For a moment, our eyes met
   ⁀ourse I turned to follow. In one window she found
     ⁀ lovely clothes
        ⁱshed…

Gone

The shock
Rocked me.
As you had been rocked by the deciding
I had to summon up the admiring.
You ran, baggage and daughter in hand
from your abuser straight to the airport. And flew away.

Ode to the Bath Plug

It used to be attached by a flimsy cord
made of tiny silver baubles,
not even a chain.
My infant fear was then,
and the worry does remain
that it could get lost.
Where would we be without the bath plug?
Searching my thoughts of those times:
as the day's play drew to a close
we children of the family
looked forward to our bathtime when
our Aunt Betty would sing us some jolly songs
and the one we often chose,
sung to a wartime tune, was
"Poor baby has gone down the plughole"
No more of it, can I recall -
no need – for that dread is lifted,
dissolved into my vision
of that dear, loving woman
our Aunt

Redemption
in response to Amanda Gorman's wonderful poem
The Hill We Climb

She says:
'But while democracy can be periodically delayed,
it can never be permanently defeated.
In this truth,
in this faith we trust.'
But Amanda, there are some reminders.
Donald Trump has just lengthened
the Nationalist list
for us to keep in our history binders.
Benito Mussolini
Francisco Franco
Adolf Hitler
Silvio Berlusconi
Ratko Mladic
Donald Trump
Boris Johnson
And so on… And on
And on
Make America Great Again?
Take Back Control?

How can we save ourselves from these men,
their easy epithets and their bullying
following?

No, we cannot forget Xi Jing Ping and Putin or his
European followers!

Sunflowers

You planted them for me
as a garden before my eyes
and when I get home I'm welcomed
by the ramp and even the building mine
all designed by my darling family and friends
for me to puzzle why? I enclose you all,
my fading garden too,
in myself: all the way from birth
and in my Van for what we're worth

29th of August 2023

Fishy February

You can't go fishing in Downing Street
Don't plaice yourself at Number Ten
Just crabbing and carping is all you'll meet
You won't catch fish, you'll only catch men

Northmoor

With the pleasant scent of cows and cow parsley
along the track towards the river
and over the Christmas-frosty, crunchy vegetation
the black dog asthma chaos cannot smell where he is.
The floodplain is filled with a bedspread of ice;
through it we can still see the soil and grass,
looking like specimens in laboratory glass.
"It's not dangerous" so hesitantly our boots
crack the canopy: we don't find keep calm and carry on.

But where is the River Thames? It has gone.
What is a river, without its banks? The brows
of philosophers will stiffen at this question.
We send a scout to find the wheres and hows.
So we skate the problem of where we walk
we tread the frozen fields with joy
and thankfully Asthmadaus returns: "Good boy".

Don't stop me

He might have been just nine years old
he had heard a song
on the radio, or one of his digital devices
and got his darling mum to get the CD,
McFly I think it was.
His favourite song struck a chord --
thumbing through our ancient collection
of cat-scratched vinyl albums
I discovered the original
Freddie Mercury of the Queen, swirling black cover,
singing Don't Stop Me Now
don't stop me at all --
the chord is still a there.

Untitled

There is a bark from Tipper: that's his form of talk
He only barks if he wants food, or a walk…
In that respect, he's like me: I only call
if I want food, or a drink, or to move. That is all

Sitting at my desk, I'm stock still
My words create a line, so I am not ill
Thoughts activate the voice box…
Hurray! I have avoided the Shingles pox.

Thames
*(Written in response to a poem about
the river Dart by Alice Oswald Thames)*

Growing up
We Found the tiny Dikler stream,
which meets the Windrush,
and runs into the heavy river Thames:
the watermill at Upper Swell
why was it staying put behind those bars?
Walking past the church, I did not know.
Nor did I know that the lake
beside which I used to sit in retreat,
around which with Kathryn I used to ride,
that it was once a millpond.

Riding amongst those hills and bridle ways
we came across a ford through
another tributary: the river Eye
to the mill at Lower Slaughter,
a name derived from *Slothre*
all meaning *Muddy Place*
(something else I did not know)

There they made bread,
devoured on our way home

Then Cotswold men arrived at dusk
with rounded platforms made from wire
"Catching crayfish luv" they said
and baiting them with smelly fish
sunk their traps into the stream.
Back next day, they found their catch
each wire world inhabited
by one, even two crustaceans
"Brill" I thought.
Since then, I wondered
"What did the crayfish think?"

A photograph reminds me
of walking three decades later, with Claire,
our children and their cousins
to a wooden bridge over the Dikler…
In turn, I am reminded of convalescence from school
with my dear mother amongst the raspberry canes.

London – 1950s

Pimlico, staying with my Aunt Betty.
Her flat had a balcony and strange furniture
and outside, trains making soot in the night.
She took us to shows – and films. I fell in love
with the South Pacific girl up the mountain
Bali Hai!
the song still goes through my mind

On Seeing Wild Goats on an Island off Mallaig

Behind us the herring boats
and sheds stiff against the shrinking hill,
as our motorboat headed west.
Gulls whooped,
Oystercatchers dipped.
Ahead, the grey sea darkened with the wind
and from it grew an island --
a cheerless place, the boatman said,
long deserted.
Perhaps its crofters hoped they might return on a better tide.
Some goats were left behind:
Still, white and wild on grassy cliffs,
their hairy progeny gazed back at us reproachfully

Xtinction Rebellion
Oxford 21 September 2019

Send not to know
for whom the bell tolls (John Donne)

We are filled the streets and spires
The school kids led the way,
the fifth form girls cheering prancing and shouting
"One two three… there is no Planet B"
their banners, T-shirts, placards tolled
The seas are rising and so are we
What I stand for is what I stand on
Make love not carbon dioxide
Inaction is a weapon of mass destruction
Act now…swim later
Be a good ancestor,
they tolled.

Milton Keynes UK
Ingram Content Group UK Ltd.
UKHW021925281024
450365UK00017B/982